Doubleday

New York   London   Toronto   Sydney   Auckland

PHOTO GRAPHS THAT CHANGED THE WORLD

The Camera as Witness

The Photograph as Evidence

LORRAINE MONK

PHOTO
GRAPHS
THAT
CHANGED
THE
WORLD

Published by Doubleday, a division of
Bantam Doubleday Dell Publishing Group, Inc.,
666 Fifth Avenue, New York, New York 10103.

Doubleday and the portrayal of an anchor
with a dolphin are trademarks of
Doubleday, a division of Bantam Doubleday Dell
Publishing Group.

Library of Congress Cataloging-in-Publication Data

Monk, Lorraine.
    Photographs that changed the world.

1. Photography, Artistic. I. Title.

TR654.M628 1989   779′.092′2   88-33595
ISBN 0-385-26195-0

This book is dedicated to all the brave, bold, intrepid photographers who were there when the world needed a witness to history. Their enduring photographs have preserved, for all of us, unforgettable moments frozen in time.

Introduction

Television, which I have served for almost forty years, is a remarkable, high-impact medium. The instantaneous transmission of pictures and sound is close to a miracle. If this miracle has a flaw, it is its lack of one important feature. This is contemplation, which motion defies. A good still photograph, studied by an enquiring mind, frequently yields more information than a mile of moving images.

Without contemplation comprehension sometimes suffers. Yesterday's motion picture newsreels and today's television newscasts have vastly increased our awareness of what our politicians and other news figures look and sound like. But by reducing their presumably cogent statements to ridiculously brief "sound bites," television has notably increased the incoherence of their pronouncements.

This distortion by compression is a by-product of our ever-accelerating world. Television's moving images flood our consciousness with the speed of the light that transmits them, leaving us benumbed and unthinking.

Interestingly, memory seems to be made up mostly of still pictures. Even when recalling loved ones, we imagine static frames, portraits, and scenes rather than people in motion. And so it is that the pictures in our minds of the great events of history are still photographs, even now in the age of television journalism.

These images, familiar to extraordinary numbers of people, have had the power to move the world in myriad ways: pictures of desperate need brought relief; photos of heroism inspired nations; pictures of politicians helped win elections.

Pictures of the poor in rural areas and city slums, and of children working in factories, sweatshops, and mines prompted remedial legislation. Pictures of the magnificence of an unspoiled western wilderness helped win support for a national park system.

Mathew Brady's portrait of Lincoln was an early demonstration of the use of photography as political propaganda. Karsh's portrait of Winston Churchill, catching his bulldog tenacity, uplifted the morale of the British people. A portrait of Sitting Bull taken eight years after the massacre at the Little Big Horn depicted a dignified chieftain and helped dispel the popular notion that Indians were bloodthirsty savages.

A screaming child, burned by napalm, running down a Vietnamese road; a South Vietnamese official firing a pistol shot into a prisoner's head on a Saigon street–these helped raise questions about the morality of a distant war.

Stop-action and stroboscopic photos of machinery and men and other living things in action have contributed substantially to our scientific and medical progress.

The moving picture, skittering across the screen, gone in an instant, is unquestionably a technological triumph. But the still photograph, rich in detail and drama, remains before us always, forever imbued with the power to provoke and inspire and move us.

WALTER CRONKITE
New York
June 1989

Preface

Photographs That Changed the World is a celebration of photography and of the dedicated men and women who devoted their lives and their genius to the compelling, tantalizing, often frustrating quest to capture an elusive image and preserve it for all the world to contemplate and enjoy.

Photography, from the moment of its invention, has been one of the most moving and powerful instruments of communication ever devised. It is not only a silent language, but also a visual language, an alphabet that the entire world can read.

The camera has been an eloquent witness to many of the momentous events of the past century and a half. And the information conveyed by photographs – the evidence they offer – has become implanted in our collective memory.

Occasionally an extraordinary photograph emerges, one that is more than the documentary record of an important event or memorable scene. The photograph itself becomes the event and, as a consequence, the world is measurably changed. The photographs presented here represent a personal selection of images that achieve this rare stature. They are not necessarily "great" photographs (although many of them are), nor even "famous" photographs (although many are immediately familiar). But every one of them has been undeniably influential. Because of them and the information they revealed, the world was ever after a different place – politically, economically, socially, morally, aesthetically, or scientifically. Or, if it cannot be said that the world was transformed, certainly people's attitudes were. Their perceptions of reality were forever altered.

The year 1989 is celebrated as the 150th anniversary of the invention of photography. The validity of any anniversary depends, of course, on when one begins counting. It is generally recognized by scholars and historians that the birth of photography actually occurred in 1826, when the French inventor Joseph Nicéphore Niépce succeeded in permanently capturing a "view from nature" on a polished pewter plate. The world's first photograph was a view from his window at his country home at Gras in central France.

At the same time, another Frenchman, Louis Jacques Mandé Daguerre, was working in Paris to perfect the process that Niépce had invented. The result of Daguerre's experiments was the beautiful silver image known as the daguerreotype, which the American writer-doctor-scientist Oliver Wendell Holmes called "the mirror with a memory."

The public announcement of the invention of the daguerreotype was made by the French Academy of Sciences on August 19, 1839, the popularly held date of birth of the photograph. In less than a decade, over two thousand cameras and half a million plates were sold in Paris alone. Enterprising publishers, anticipating the profits to be made from travel books containing reproductions of daguerreotype views, sent photographers to exotic, faraway places – Egypt, Russia, North Africa, and North America. Millions of people rushed to have their portraits taken. Families acquired pictorial records of their lives and, in time, those of a long parade of ancestors, lovingly preserved in ornate albums.

The delicate tones of the silver daguerreotype and its amazing detail were greatly admired. It inspired the French painter Paul Delaroche to declare, upon seeing a daguerreotype for the first time, "From today, painting is dead." Whether painting was dead, dying, or merely changing, there can be no doubt that the invention of photography had a profound effect on the artists of the second half of the nineteenth century and an even greater impact on the direction of modern art in the twentieth century. Its contribution to the communications revolution in our time cannot be overstated.

Photography touches all our lives in many ways. The following pages contain photographs that have had a dramatic impact on the world and, in a myriad of subtle, inescapable ways, upon all of us.

LORRAINE MONK
Toronto
June 1989

Acknowledgements

Some years ago Jack McClelland and I were having a pleasant late-night dinner in a Toronto restaurant. I was eager to impress upon the prestigious publisher (frequently described in Canada as a "national treasure") the incredible power of photography and how essential it was for him to join the board of the Canadian Museum of Photography, which I was struggling to establish. It was close to 2 A.M., the restaurant manager wanted to close, and tired waiters hovered around our table, eyes pleading us to leave. I called upon the strongest argument I could muster. "Do you realize, Jack, that there are, quite literally, photographs that have changed the world?" Slowly he put his glass down. He looked directly at me. "Lorraine, that is the greatest title I have ever heard. You must write that book." I settled down to do just that, and Jack became a trustee of the museum. All in all, a good evening.

From the beginning, the designer of my choice for the book was John Lee. I was delighted when, in spite of his heavy schedule, he agreed to work with me once again. My admiration for his unerring sense of style and elegance is boundless. As always his technical advice and artistic guidance have been invaluable.

Jan Walter, my Canadian publisher, took the text in hand with a firm but gentle embrace. Her unshakable patience can be summed up in one word – awesome.

John Duff, who shepherded the book along its sometimes rocky path on behalf of Doubleday, kept my spirits bright by his steadfast belief in the work.

Canapress Photo Service, Toronto, and especially Stan Mulcahey and John Beaton, were relentless in their pursuit of obscure photographs.

David Beckstead, that rare breed, a protective, caring bank manager, was always there when I needed him.

Everyone at D. W. Friesen & Sons committed themselves to an effort "above and beyond" the norm as they wrestled to make the reproductions in this book as beautiful as the originals. It was a joy to work with people so able and so committed. A special thanks to Bob Hamilton, who never doubted that some of my flamboyant ideas were capable of translation into sparkling reality. And to Mary Black and her staff at Colour Technologies, who prepared the separations with skill and sensitivity, my warmest appreciation for their dedication to this project.

To Nancy Smith – friend, confidante, secretary, researcher, holder of hand in dark moments – I am especially grateful. Without her it would not have been possible to complete this book on schedule. Nancy was the one indispensable ingredient in this entire project.

I was delighted when Walter Cronkite, the indefatigable journalist who has been a reliable and trusted witness to much of the history of our time, agreed to contribute the introduction. For his perceptive and glowing tribute to the power of photography, he has my deepest thanks.

Many other people helped in many ways. Friends, family, and colleagues have responded generously to calls upon their time and ideas. To all I acknowledge my indebtedness. Each, in a variety of special ways, played a part in the making of this book.

The Photographs

1 View of the Courtyard at Gras
Joseph Nicéphore Niépce

2 Latticed Window, Lacock Abbey
William Henry Fox Talbot

3 Boulevard du Temple, Paris
Louis Jacques Mandé Daguerre

4 Colossus of Ramses II, Egypt
Maxime Du Camp

5 Aerial View of Paris
Nadar

6 Abraham Lincoln
Mathew B. Brady

7 Mrs. Herbert Duckworth
Julia Margaret Cameron

8 Old Faithful
William Henry Jackson

9 Galloping Horse
Eadweard J. Muybridge

10 Chief Sitting Bull
William Notman

11 Gathering Water-lilies
Peter Henry Emerson

12 George Eastman with Kodak Camera
Frederick Fargo Church

13 Underwater Self-portrait
Louis Boutan

14 Child Spinner
Lewis W. Hine

15 Charlie Chaplin
Motion picture still

16 Charles Lindbergh and the *Spirit of St. Louis*
Photographer unknown

17 Greta Garbo
Clarence Sinclair Bull

18 Drop of Milk
Harold E. Edgerton

19 Sharecropper Family, Alabama
Walker Evans

20 Migrant Mother
Dorothea Lange

21 Jesse Owens
Photographer unknown

22 Death of a Loyalist Soldier
Robert Capa

23 The Bombing of Guernica
Photographer unknown

24 Franklin Delano Roosevelt
Photographer unknown

25 Pearl Harbor
Unidentified U.S. Navy Photographer

26 Winston Spencer Churchill
Yousuf Karsh

27 The Warsaw Ghetto Uprising
From the files of SS Commander Jürgen Stroop

28 D Day
Gilbert A. Milne

29 Raising the Flag at Iwo Jima
Joe Rosenthal

30 The Living Dead of Buchenwald
Margaret Bourke-White

31 Anne Frank
Self-portrait

32 First Atomic Bomb Explosion
Los Alamos National Laboratory

33 The Walk to Paradise Garden
W. Eugene Smith

34 Gandhi
Margaret Bourke-White

35 Unidentified Flying Object
Paul Trent

36 Marilyn Monroe
Matthew Zimmerman

37 Ranch Market
Robert Frank

38 Mao Tse-tung
Official portrait

39 Cuban Missile Base
U.S. Air Force

40 The March on Washington
Robert W. Kelley

41 John Fitzgerald Kennedy, Jr.
Harry Leder

42 Execution of a Viet Cong Suspect
Eddie Adams

43 Shooting at Kent State University
John Filo

44 South Vietnamese Children Burned by Napalm
Nick (Huynh Cong) Ut

45 Tomoko in Her Bath
W. Eugene Smith

46 Terry Fox
Gail Harvey

47 Edwin "Buzz" Aldrin on the Moon
Neil Armstrong

48 Harp Seal Pup
Fred Bruemmer

49 The *Challenger* Explodes
NASA

50 The Statue of Liberty
Aram Gesar

51 Earthrise
William Anders

The invention of photography was the inevitable climax of a long love affair between science and art. Pursued for centuries, the dream of what photography could accomplish had existed since ancient times, the impulse rooted in man's urge to record his direct observations and make permanent his visual knowledge. But the dream remained as elusive as it was fascinating.

The Greek philosopher Aristotle was familiar with the phenomenon of the camera obscura (literally "dark room") and the great Renaissance master Leonardo da Vinci described its properties. Both knew the principle: that light entering a minute hole in the wall of a darkened room or box forms on the opposite wall an inverted image of whatever lies outside.

In 1568, Professor Danielo Barbaro, working at the University of Padua, demonstrated that a clearer image could be produced if a lens was substituted for the pinhole. Gradually the camera obscura became standard equipment for artists. In 1764, Count Francesco Algarotti devoted an entire chapter in his book on painting to the value of the apparatus, pointing out that the great Italian painters could not have represented nature so accurately without it.

Some historians have wondered why photography was not invented earlier than it was. In 1725, the German physicist Johann Heinrich Schulze had established that silver salts are radically altered by exposure to light. The essential ingredient needed to capture the fleeting image created by the camera had been identified. But it would be another hundred years before these long understood optical and chemical phenomena were brought together to produce the miracle that we now call a photograph.

The distinction of being "the world's first photographer" fell to a Frenchman, Joseph Nicéphore Niépce. On May 5, 1816, he described his efforts in a letter to his brother: "I placed the apparatus in the room where I work, facing the birdhouse and the open casement. I made the experiment according to the process which you know and I saw on the white paper all that part of the birdhouse which is seen from the window and a faint image of the casement." Niépce regarded his experiment as "an imperfect trial," but he persisted with great diligence and ingenuity. Some believe he may have succeeded in making a permanent image in 1822, but the "heliograph," as he called it (from the Greek for "sun" or "light"), has not survived.

In 1826, he was more successful. He coated a polished pewter plate with bitumen of Judea, then treated the plate with a solution of oil of lavender and turpentine after it had been exposed to light. The exposure time was an exhausting eight hours. The result was the ghostly image reproduced here, which authorities recognize as the world's oldest existing photograph.

While Niépce never solved the problem of making multiple images, his creation of a permanent image was fundamental to the development of photography. From this first, blurry photograph the visual-communications revolution could mark its shaky but felicitous beginning.

In 1933, the one-hundredth anniversary of Niépce's death, the government of France erected a monument to his memory at St.-Loup-de-Varennes. The inscription on the imposing stone memorial reads simply:

Dans ce village
Nicéphore Niépce
inventa la photographie
en 1822

1826
VIEW OF THE COURTYARD AT GRAS, FRANCE

JOSEPH NICÉPHORE NIÉPCE / FRENCH 1765–1833

William Henry Fox Talbot was an inquisitive English gentleman of comfortable means with an astonishing range of interests from linguistics to science. By the age of thirty-three, he had published twelve papers on his mathematical and optical observations, had been elected a member of Parliament, and was taking the mandatory grand tour of Europe. While thus at leisure, he experimented with a camera obscura to capture "fairy pictures, creations of a moment and destined as rapidly to fade away." It was during these travels that the thought occurred to him "how charming it would be if it were possible to cause these natural images to imprint themselves durably, and remain fixed upon the paper! And why should it not be possible? I asked myself."

Immediately upon his return to England, Talbot turned his attention to the problem. Working with a tiny two-and-a-half-inch-square camera, Talbot sensitized a piece of writing paper and exposed it for over an hour. The delicate, lilac-tinted sheet of paper he then removed from his camera is today acclaimed as the world's first negative. The image was not more than one inch square, but its creator proudly wrote in the space beside it that it was so sharp "the squares of glafs [*sic*] about 200 in number could be counted, with the help of a lens." The renowned British astronomer Sir John Herschel coined the words "negative" and "positive" to describe the process. Herschel, intrigued by the search to find a simple way to render lasting images, had contributed a vital discovery of his own: that sodium thiosulfate (hypo) was the best fixing agent for making photographs permanent.

Talbot's invention of the negative-positive technique made possible the creation of multiple prints from a single negative, thus changing the course of photographic history. Without this technique, modern photography as we understand it today would be impossible. On January 31, 1839, Talbot announced his discovery to the world in a paper he read before the Royal Society in London. Three weeks later he followed it with a second paper in which he described all of the technical details necessary to duplicate his experiments.

Five years later he achieved another historic first. He published a collection of his own photographs in an exquisite and rare book he called *The Pencil of Nature*. Today it is one of the prizes most sought after by the ever-growing community of eager photography collectors, who hail it as the world's first photographic book. In the almost century and a half since the publication of *The Pencil of Nature*, a virtual avalanche of photography books has been sold in countries worldwide, serving a market of avid readers and an even more avid following of photographers. Whether amateur or professional, most strive for – and some succeed in achieving – the sublime standards set by one of photography's illustrious pioneers, William Henry Fox Talbot.

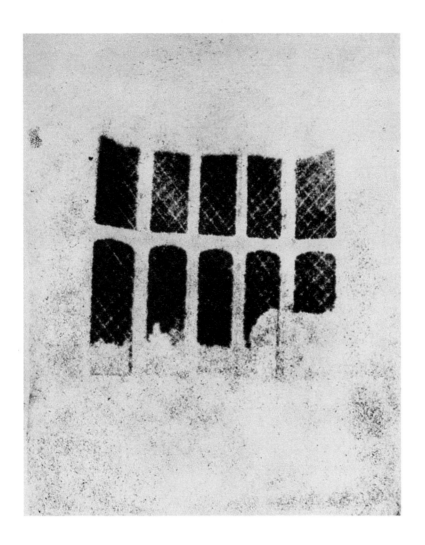

1835
LATTICED WINDOW, LACOCK ABBEY, ENGLAND

WILLIAM HENRY FOX TALBOT / ENGLISH 1800–1877

Louis Jacques Mandé Daguerre was destined to achieve both fame and fortune as the man who is most widely regarded as the "inventor" of photography. Certainly he did give photography its first practical application. After the invention of the daguerreotype, the grip of photography on the public mind and imagination never lost its hold.

As so often happens in new fields of endeavor, a number of talented individuals were wrestling simultaneously with the idea of capturing images from nature and rendering them permanent. And as so often happens too, one man leaves his name on a discovery or an idea which is in fact the result of cumulative effort by many brilliant minds. The man who gave his name to a process, a product, and a period was Daguerre.

Recognizing that the experiments of Niépce were fundamental to the development of his own ideas, Daguerre formed a partnership with the ailing inventor in 1829. Four years later Niépce died and his son, Isidore, took his place as Daguerre's partner. Early in 1839, a supporter of Daguerre, astronomer and physicist Dominique François Arago, demonstrated their invention – the daguerreotype – before the French Academy of Sciences. Daguerre was awarded an annual appropriation of six thousand francs and the young Niépce an annuity of four thousand francs. In return, the two inventors were to "place in the hands of the Ministry of the Interior a sealed package containing the history and most detailed and exact description of the invention."

On August 19, 1839, Arago made public the technical details of the daguerreotype, declaring: "France has adopted this discovery and from the first has shown her pride in being able to donate it generously to the whole world." Daguerre promptly published a seventy-nine-page booklet describing the process at length. The public's reaction was one of wild enthusiasm. Opticians' shops throughout Paris were besieged with excited amateurs clamoring to buy the necessary daguerreotype apparatus. Word of the fabulous invention spread quickly, and within months Daguerre's pamphlet had been translated and reproduced in thirty editions and distributed in a score of cities, among them London, Edinburgh, New York, Paris, Philadelphia, and Madrid. Even in faraway Russia, St. Petersburg wanted copies.

The daguerreotype reproduced here, made in 1839, claimed a unique distinction. It is heralded as the first photograph to capture the image, however faint, of a human being. Early daguerreotypes required exposures of varying lengths depending on the strength of the sun and the time of day. On this memorable day, the Boulevard du Temple was far from empty, as the photograph suggests. Strolling pedestrians and clattering carriages simply moved too quickly for their images to be recorded. The anonymous gentleman having his boots shined stood still just long enough for Daguerre to capture his outline in this now famous cityscape. The fastidious Parisian achieved immortality as the first human being ever to have his picture taken.

Soon formal portraits were much in demand. Just a few months after Daguerre's announcement, the American inventor Samuel F. B. Morse succeeded in making one of the world's first daguerreotype portraits. In reporting his triumph, Morse described how his wife and daughter sat "from ten to twenty minutes... on the roof of a building, in the full sunlight, with the eyes closed." The process was excruciating for all concerned. Within a year vast improvements had been made. Photographic studios proliferated as the world rushed to have its picture taken – probably one of the most pleasant and most harmless pastimes ever indulged.

1839
BOULEVARD DU TEMPLE, PARIS

LOUIS JACQUES MANDÉ DAGUERRE / FRENCH 1787–1851

In the early days they were called simply "traveling men," for many of those who set out to record the wonders of the world did not consider themselves photographers only. They were first and foremost explorers of the global landscape, writers (often with an archaeological fascination), mountain climbers, or curiosity seekers. Robust health was the first prerequisite. Strong backs and even stronger nerves were paramount. Devilishly heavy loads of camera equipment and bulky camping necessities had to be hauled up mountain peaks or across desert sands. Only the most fearless succeeded: the Bisson Frères, who set out from Paris to conquer the Alps; the French-born Felice Beaton, who set off from England to photograph in India, China, and Japan; Francis Frith of London, who traveled to Egypt and the Holy Land, where he exposed his fragile sixteen- by twenty-inch glass plates amid extreme conditions of heat and dust; and the Australian Henry Beaufoy Merlin, who captured Sydney Harbor in astonishing detail on one of the largest wet-plate negatives ever made – five feet by three and a half feet.

One of the first to go in search of Egyptian antiquities was the French writer Maxime Du Camp. He set about learning how to take pictures so that he could document a trip which he would make in company with his good friend and fellow writer Gustave Flaubert. In November 1849, they undertook an archaeological mission to Greece, Asia Minor, and the Middle East that would occupy them until 1851. Du Camp sardonically recounted that the taking of pictures was a relatively simple affair, but transporting the equipment by mule, camel, or human porters was an altogether more difficult matter.

In 1852, his extraordinary photographs were published in a much sought-after book: *Egypte, Nubie, Palestine et Syrie*. It sparked keen interest in archaeology and an even keener interest in foreign travel. Those who could, did; those who preferred not to, sat back in their comfortable armchairs and let a growing army of photographers make the perilous voyages for them. Braving terrible heat, intense cold, insects, illness, and danger, these adventurers marched off to little-known and exotic places, then returned laden with photographic treasures to be enjoyed and studied in the sedate privacy of one's own home.

Readers gazed with awe at photographs from around the world: the Pyramids of Egypt, the thundering Niagara Falls in Upper Canada, the bazaars of the Orient. It was the indefatigable, peripatetic photographer who would first bind all of humanity in the shared delight of the world's geographic and cultural wonders.

Travel photography inevitably whetted the appetites of millions to take up a camera and travel also. Even the most timid thrill seekers were propelled out of their chairs to join an eager band of tourists swarming over the globe. Photographic safaris became popular, and soon photographs replaced the stuffed lion and tiger heads mounted over fireplaces in Victorian parlors. The photograph became the ultimate testimonial, the coveted trophy.

1850
COLOSSUS OF RAMSES II AT ABU SIMBEL, EGYPT

MAXIME DU CAMP / FRENCH 1822–1894

A man of many talents, Gaspard-Félix Tournachon – or Nadar, as he preferred to be called – was an adventurer, bohemian, balloonist, caricaturist, political activist, and exceptionally talented photographer. He mingled with the writers, artists, and intellectuals of Paris during the time of Napoleon III, and he photographed many of them with great skill and sensitivity. Edouard Manet, Jean Baptiste Camille Corot, Alexandre Dumas, Charles Pierre Baudelaire, Eugène Delacroix, Honoré Daumier, George Sand, and Sarah Bernhardt were just a few of the famous individuals who sat for him.

Nadar had worked to combine his ballooning skills with his photographic interest for several years, but he was constantly frustrated in his efforts by gas escaping from the balloon and caking the collodion on his photographic plates. Dozens of times he attempted to make an aerial photograph, struggling to coat and develop his plates in a makeshift darkroom while he floated at dizzying heights over Paris.

It was not until 1858 that he achieved his first success. Hovering at an altitude of 520 meters (1,600 feet), he captured the world's first view of a city from the air and the distinction of being the world's first aerial photographer.

One of his admirers, Honoré Daumier, was so delighted with Nadar's achievement that he produced an amusing cartoon to mark the occasion: "Nadar Raising Photography to the Height of Art." Nadar was only mildly amused. "There is," he once said, "no such thing as art photography. . . . There are only people who know how to see and others who don't even know how to look."

To the modern traveler, accustomed to observing the earth from the high-flying altitudes of today's jet aircraft, Nadar's view of Paris may seem somewhat mundane. But among people of the mid-nineteenth century, most of whom had never viewed the world from anything higher than a treetop, this panorama of one of the great capitals created a sensation. It offered a bird's-eye view of a city that held a romantic fascination for its earthbound citizens – and for tens of thousands more around the world, who merely fantasized about the city that even then was admired as one of the most glamorous in Europe.

1858
AERIAL VIEW OF PARIS

NADAR / FRENCH 1820–1910

Abraham Lincoln is a man imprisoned in a myth. And the myth has been given substance and credibility by the many photographs made of him during his brief and turbulent political career. As the embattled Civil War president, he grappled with the painful issue of slavery and the awesome prospect of secession. When an assassin's bullet ended his life on April 15, 1865, he was elevated instantly to the rank of tragic hero. And history has subsequently conferred an enduring sainthood upon him.

He is revered as the greatest American who ever lived and the quintessential folk hero. One historian went so far as to suggest it might have been a sacrilege to photograph him, since, like the gods, Abe Lincoln should merely be "perceived," not photographed.

Although he often alluded to himself as homely, he enjoyed being photographed. He was a frequent and willing visitor to photographic studios; indeed, he may have been the first politician in history to recognize the compelling power of the photograph to win votes and influence people. Certainly, he was the first American president to be extensively photographed; in all, over 130 daguerreotypes, tintypes, ambrotypes, stereographic cards, cartes de visite, and official portraits were made of him, of which 120 survive.

One of the finest portraits, and without doubt the most influential, was this one taken by Mathew Brady in his New York studio on February 27, 1860. Lincoln was still dressed in the attire he wore for his now famous Cooper Union speech delivered earlier in the day ("Let us have faith that right makes might, and in that faith, let us, to the end, dare to do our duty as we understand it."). The fifty-one-year-old presidential candidate would later proclaim, upon his election to the White House, "Brady and the Cooper Union speech made me president of the United States." Since the photograph was widely circulated during the campaign, both in the illustrated press and through the enormously popular Currier and Ives prints, it is probable that a great many more people saw and were persuaded by the photograph than ever heard the Cooper Union speech.

Even Brady himself seems to have sensed that he had captured some special essence of the man on film. Later he would confide to his friend, the portrait painter Francis Carpenter, that he too believed that his photograph of Lincoln was "the means of his election." Thus this picture is recognized as the first successful publicity photograph in history.

Down through the years, in countless political campaigns worldwide, publicity managers would fret over the image their candidate projected on film. A face that "the camera loves" has come to be regarded as a distinct advantage for those contemplating a political career.

1860
ABRAHAM LINCOLN

MATHEW B. BRADY / AMERICAN 1823–1896

Julia Margaret Cameron left her indelible mark on the richly layered world of Victorian England. Born in Calcutta, she married a senior British bureaucrat, bore six children, and went to live in England in 1848. Her children had all departed the family home and she was approaching fifty – elderly for a Victorian woman – when she was given the gift of a camera by her daughter with the endearing message "It may amuse you, Mother, to try to photograph during your solitude at Fresh Water."

And amuse Julia Margaret Cameron it did. Photography became the consuming passion of her life, and, by her own description, she handled her lens "with a tender ardor." She photographed her family and she photographed her friends, many of them the "eminent Victorians" of their day: Thomas Carlyle, Sir John Herschel, Charles Darwin, Robert Browning, and the poet laureate of England, Alfred Lord Tennyson. "When I have such men before my camera," she wrote, "my whole soul has endeavoured to do its duty towards them in recording faithfully the greatness of the inner as well as the features of the outer man."

Mrs. Cameron worshiped beauty, and one of her favorite models was her niece Julia, undoubtedly named in honor of her eccentric aunt, and by any standard a great beauty. The niece married twice, first to Herbert Duckworth, who died leaving her with three children. In 1878, she married Sir Leslie Stephen and produced four more children. Her youngest daughter would be celebrated as one of England's greatest writers, Virginia Woolf.

Mrs. Cameron was a pioneer in demonstrating that women – even nineteenth-century women, hampered by hoopskirts and Victorian perceptions of propriety – could master the challenge of photography if they were not deterred by its cumbersome equipment, by the unladylike fumes that clung to their hair, or by the nasty chemical stains that tarnished their fingers. The redoubtable Mrs. Cameron was not easily stopped by anything. Sixty-five years before her illustrious great-niece, Virginia, published a witty essay vividly explaining to women the importance of having "a room of one's own," Julia Margaret Cameron decreed that freedom was a photographic room of one's own. She energetically converted a chicken coop into a studio and an unused coal house into a darkroom.

Julia Margaret Cameron's bequest to Virginia Woolf was manifold: the vibrant example of her free spirit, her independence, her desire to see beneath the surface of things. And she left Virginia an album of exquisite photographs of her mother, whose death when Virginia was thirteen years old permanently clouded her life. The description of the beautiful Mrs. Ramsay in her novel *To the Lighthouse* is based on Virginia Woolf's remembrance of her mother, no doubt refreshed by her great-aunt's enduring portraits, including this one which captures a woman of extraordinary radiance and grace.

Julia Margaret Cameron's legacy benefited not only her family and heirs. She inspired generations of women to break the silken bonds of a restrictive femininity, to pick up a camera and to record the world around them. Today, Mrs. Cameron's work is acclaimed as among the greatest portrait photography ever produced. For the many women photographers who have traveled the path she cleared for them, we can only guess at the magnitude of their indebtedness to this indefatigable Victorian lady.

1867
MRS. HERBERT DUCKWORTH

JULIA MARGARET CAMERON / ENGLISH 1815–1879

William Henry Jackson devoted most of his long life to the pursuit of his first love, photography. When he died in 1942 at the age of ninety-nine, he was mourned as the last of the great frontier photographers.

In 1870, Dr. Ferdinand V. Hayden of the U.S. Geological Survey hired Jackson as photographer for a three-month expedition in the American West. Jackson enjoyed the work, took some outstanding photographs of the breathtaking scenery, and had a dry gorge on the North Platte River named Jackson Canyon in his honor.

The following year, in 1871, Dr. Hayden persuaded Jackson to join his team on an expedition to the Yellowstone area of Wyoming. Jackson packed an eight- by ten-inch camera, a stereo camera (stereo views were becoming extremely popular), and two hundred pounds of additional photographic equipment. Fortunately, he was accompanied on the trek by a very trustworthy and tireless mule. On a later trip, in 1875, he carried a twenty- by twenty-four-inch camera – the largest plates ever used on a field trip in North America. He felt the extra burden was worth it to demonstrate to his fellow Americans the extraordinary grandeur of the mountains and wilderness scenery – grandeur which, he believed, smaller cameras "cannot possibly impart."

Jackson's employer, Dr. Hayden, was a man of great vision and determination, and he possessed an acute appreciation of the power of photography. His goal was to protect America's wilderness from commercial exploitation and private gain by preserving its fragile beauty for all Americans, including future generations.

Realizing that cold geological reports filled with endless statistics and charts might not have the desired effect on the federal government, Hayden decided to produce a photographic album of nine of Jackson's powerful images, including the most dramatic photograph of all, "Old Faithful." Every member of the House and Senate received a beautifully bound, gold-embossed volume. Needless to say, the bill to create Yellowstone National Park, the foundation of the National Park System, passed by a good margin. President Ulysses S. Grant signed it into law on March 1, 1872.

America's awareness of its priceless wilderness heritage was aroused, and the attractions of the national parks created in the years following became central features of the country's travel and holiday plans.

Millions of photographs of Old Faithful have since been taken (the great master Ansel Adams photographed it on three different occasions), but none were more influential than Jackson's 1871 picture and, some would claim, none more beautiful.

1871
OLD FAITHFUL, YELLOWSTONE NATIONAL PARK, WYOMING

WILLIAM HENRY JACKSON / AMERICAN 1843–1942

Eadweard Muybridge emigrated to America in his early twenties and soon made a reputation for himself as a landscape photographer of exceptional talent and sensibility. He was working in California, concentrating his efforts on the Yosemite area, when a former governor of California, Leland Stanford, asked him to use his photographic skills to settle a dispute between Stanford and a friend.

Contrary to popular belief at the time, Stanford believed that at a certain point in a full gallop, a horse lifted all four feet off the ground. Conventional wisdom held that even at full speed, a horse would have one foot touching the ground.

Leland Stanford had bet a friend twenty-five thousand dollars that the traditional view was wrong, and he hired Muybridge to settle the matter. Muybridge made his first attempt to photograph a fast-moving horse in 1872, but due to the limitations of the equipment available at the time, the results were inconclusive. Six years later, in June 1878, Stanford again commissioned Muybridge to photograph his beautiful, fast mare, Sallie Gardner. Leland Stanford was convinced he was right and he wanted the documentary evidence to prove it. The event was staged in San Francisco and the press was invited to witness the historic occasion. Muybridge set up twelve cameras, all attached to fine black threads that were strung across the track at strategic locations. When Sallie Gardner's breast hit the black threads, the shutters were released.

To everyone's delight and to some people's surprise, the photographs proved conclusively that at a certain point in a full gallop – frame number three shown here – all four feet of a horse are clearly off the ground, bunched together under the belly. Artists and the public now had to acknowledge that observation with the human eye could not compare with the unerring vision of the camera. The history of the now familiar racetrack photo finish got its start that June day in San Francisco. The photographer, intrigued by such experiments, went on to devote the rest of his life to a prolific photographic study of human and animal locomotion, the results of which were quickly seized upon by painters, physiologists, scientists, and engineers who considered his work an invaluable aid to their own.

On May 14, 1880, Muybridge again made history when his photographs of a galloping horse were shown at the California School of Fine Arts in San Francisco. The images were projected on a large screen with a special lantern – a "zoogyroscope." The projector used two glass disks: one carrying twelve images revolving in one direction, and a second, slotted disk that revolved in the opposite direction and that served as a shutter. The effect of a running horse was so realistic that a reporter who covered the event wrote, "The only thing missing was the clatter of hoofs."

With a series of still photographs, Muybridge had created the world's first motion picture.

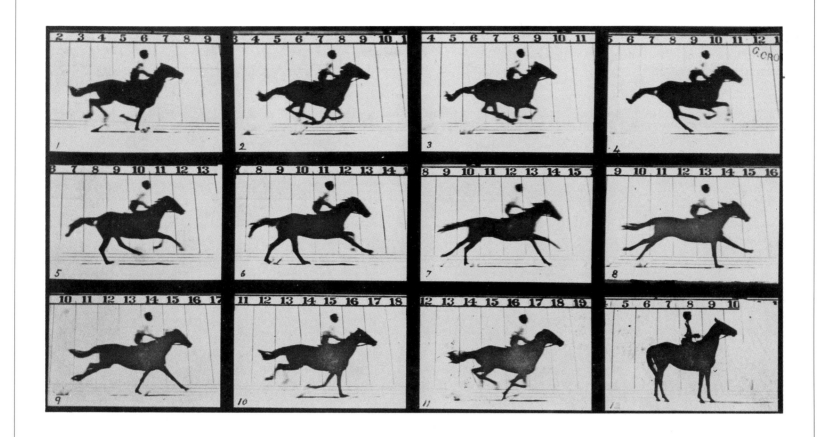

1878
GALLOPING HORSE

EADWEARD J. MUYBRIDGE / AMERICAN 1830–1904

This commanding portrait of Sitting Bull was made by William Notman at his Montreal studio in 1885. Nine years earlier the charismatic chief had achieved both fame and infamy for his role in annihilating General George Custer and his entire cavalry unit at the Battle of the Little Big Horn in Montana, a battle colorfully referred to by historians as "Custer's last stand." Fleeing to refuge in Canada, Sitting Bull had declared philosophically as he crossed into Saskatchewan, "The meat of the buffalo tastes the same on both sides of the border."

Notman had opened his photography gallery in 1856 to meet the growing demand for portraits by Montrealers and the international celebrities who flocked to his studio. The reverse side of his photographs, prized collector's items today, were handsomely decorated with the inscription "W. Notman – Photographer to Her Majesty." The reigning monarch, Queen Victoria – who along with her consort, Prince Albert, took an immense delight in photography – acquired numerous Notman prints for the royal collection at Buckingham Palace.

Notman was a photographer recognized not only for his considerable technical skill, but also for the ceaseless curiosity with which he, his sons, and his studio employees traveled the vast country around them. With their cherished cameras they journeyed far and wide, from the historic seaports of the Atlantic to the remote Pacific coast. Notman's immense photographic records – almost 400,000 prints bear the studio's imprint – comprise a sweeping portrait of North America during the Victorian era.

Not content merely to photograph the rich and the powerful of the cities, Notman dispatched members of his staff to the great plains of the prairies, where they photographed the Cree Indians and the Blackfoot of Alberta with the same devotion to capturing an individual's unique character and personality that they employed in photographing princes and prime ministers.

One of his greatest contributions to our understanding of the past lies in this abundant and sensitive documentation of Indian life in North America. As the end of the nineteenth century approached, most of the great nomadic Indian nations had been reduced to a shadow of their former glory. Most of their lands had been taken from them, the plains were being settled by newcomers, the buffalo herds had been virtually destroyed, and once proud Indian tribes had been crushed by starvation, disease, rifle fire, and cannon.

The ancient traditions of these native people began fading into mist and myth. Only a few photographers bothered to salute their passing, foremost among them Edward Sheriff Curtis and Adam Clark Vroman in the United States, and William Notman in Canada. They knew they were working against time in their efforts to record a people and a way of life that were vanishing.

The photographs of the Notman studio and of Notman's American contemporaries have had a profound impact on North America's appreciation of its native people. The cruel stereotype of Indians as "savages" has gradually given way to a new understanding of native North Americans as a people of great dignity, possessed of an enormously rich and varied culture.

This magnificent photograph of the great Sioux chief was to become one of Notman's most widely acclaimed pictures. Postcards bearing Sitting Bull's image were distributed worldwide and the famous face appeared on millions of matchboxes, calendars, and other popular items. For most North Americans, and countless others around the world, photographs such as this one are the way they will remember, not without sorrow, North America's founding race.

1885
CHIEF SITTING BULL

WILLIAM NOTMAN / CANADIAN 1826–1891

Is photography art? The question has been debated with varying degrees of intensity and passion for more than a century. The issue attracted wide public attention in March 1886, when Peter Henry Emerson spoke to a camera club in London on the subject "Photography – A Pictorial Art." A few months later, he stirred up the discussion again by submitting his platinum print "Gathering Water-lilies" to a London salon as "a work of art."

Three years later Emerson developed his controversial aesthetic theories in a textbook entitled *Naturalistic Photography*. It was promptly labeled "a bombshell dropped in a tea party," and the critics rushed to take sides.

Curiously, in January 1891, Emerson dramatically reversed the position he had so passionately defended. In a black-bordered pamphlet, "The Death of Naturalistic Photography," he declared that following a series of lengthy conversations with a great painter, whom he was not at liberty to identify, he had renounced his previously held beliefs. He had erred, he confessed, in stating that photography could be art. His dismal confession was elaborately presented in the final chapter of the third edition of *Naturalistic Photography*, under the heading "Photography – Not Art." Photography was a very minor art, he concluded, if indeed it could be called art at all.

But his repudiation and denial came too late to stop the debate. The seed had been sown, and the arguments, pro and con, would resound well into the 1980s. Emerson's original position was adopted by, among others, the Vienna Camera Club, which in 1891 held an exhibition of photographs presented as works of art, and by the great American photographer Alfred Stieglitz, who fought tirelessly and ultimately successfully to ensure photography's acceptance as an art. In the end, of course, photography was not only accepted as art, but transcended the status of "minor" art to become one of the most powerful art forms of the twentieth century.

Today, the attitude of many is relatively casual and simple: if it hangs in an art gallery, it must be art! If this is so, the battle was won long ago in 1896, when the U.S. National Museum in Washington purchased fifty photographs from a "Washington Salon and Photographic Art Exhibition." The price paid for all fifty pictures was three hundred dollars. The photographs were to hang in the institution's permanent collection, an acquisition that is believed to have been the first recorded museum purchase of photographs as works of art.

1886
GATHERING WATER-LILIES

PETER HENRY EMERSON / ENGLISH 1856–1936

Although there had been an astonishing variety of small cameras developed in the 1880s, it was not until George Eastman introduced the Kodak in 1888 that the mass appeal of photography seized America and Europe and thereafter spread quickly to the far corners of the earth. Eastman called his now famous camera the Kodak for no particular reason except that he liked the word. It was easy to remember and could be pronounced in any language.

But Eastman's creative brilliance went beyond the invention of a new camera. He pioneered a fast, efficient photo-finishing system that took the tedium and guesswork out of photography and made picture taking fun.

The original Kodak box camera measured 3¹/₄ inches by 3³/₄ inches by 6¹/₂ inches with a fixed-focus lens. Its rolled film, enough for one hundred pictures, was loaded into the camera at the factory. The cost to the consumer was twenty-five dollars, including film and processing. When the photographer had exposed all the film, the entire camera was sent to the Kodak plant in Rochester, New York. The pictures were printed, and the camera reloaded and returned to the owner for ten dollars. The simplicity of the process, promoted with the catchy advertising slogan "You press the button, we do the rest," brought the pleasure and excitement of photography to the masses.

An immediate consequence of Eastman's invention was a blizzard of amateur photographs that soon became known as snapshots. The word was borrowed from hunters' jargon. When a hunter fired a gun from the hip, without taking careful aim, it was described as a snap shot. Photographers referred to the process of taking pictures as shooting, and they would take pride in a good day's shoot the way country gentlemen would boast about the number of birds brought down in an afternoon.

The Kodak made photography not only easy but fun. Almost overnight photography became one of the world's most popular hobbies. A new and ubiquitous folk art was born; the showing of one's latest pictures and the creation of family albums became popular social pastimes. Camera clubs and associations numbered their members in the millions. One ardent amateur was the French novelist Emile Zola, who took innumerable photographs of his family, friends, and travels. Interviewed about his favorite hobby in 1900, he observed, "In my opinion you cannot say you have thoroughly seen anything until you have got a photograph of it."

"The little black box," as the Kodak was affectionately dubbed, revolutionized the way people communicated. "A picture is worth a thousand words" was the claim and there were literally billions of pictures. In one year alone – 1988, the centenary of the invention of the Kodak – it is estimated that close to thirty billion pictures were taken worldwide. Half of these – fifteen billion – were taken in the United States alone. The impact of the sale of photographic equipment on the economy is equally mind-boggling.

Photography has played an essential role in the media revolution. It has vastly enhanced our ability to convey information, so that the concept of the global village has become a commonplace. Photographs have immeasurably extended our understanding of and compassion for our fellow human beings.

Did Mr. Eastman have the faintest idea of the power residing in his "little black box"?

1890
GEORGE EASTMAN WITH KODAK CAMERA

FREDERICK FARGO CHURCH / AMERICAN 1864–1925

13

Photography and science have forged an amazingly fruitful partnership in many areas of endeavor – none more so than in the exploration of oceans, which have fascinated man since the dawn of time. Ancient seafaring peoples developed colorful legends and strange myths about the sea. Monsters, gods, and a multitude of curious creatures inhabited the shadowy depths; seductive sirens lured the unsuspecting to watery graves. The mystery of what lies beneath the waves has intrigued the intrepid for centuries.

Diving bells, underwater suits, and even primitive submarines were in existence as early as the sixteenth century. But it was not until the late nineteenth century that the oceans came to be perceived and explored as the last frontiers on planet earth. Jealously guarding its secrets, teeming with life and boundless resources, the ocean became a magnificent challenge, even an obsession, to those with the courage, the skill, and the ingenuity to probe its waters.

The first recorded scientific underwater expedition was led by a distinguished zoology professor from the Sorbonne in Paris, Dr. Henri Milne-Edwards. The year was 1844; the place was the Strait of Messina, off Italy. Using a diving helmet supplied with compressed air pumped from the surface, the professor studied marine animals in their natural habitat and brought back amazing stories of strange, never-before-seen creatures of exotic, iridescent beauty.

Twelve years later, in 1856, an Englishman, William Thompson, struggled with makeshift equipment to make the world's first underwater photograph. It was a blurry, ill-defined image of sand and seaweed. While it was a remarkable achievement, the image was not considered a success.

In 1893, French zoologist Louis Boutan experimented with an underwater camera and produced a number of clear and more enduring images. One of the most delightful is this 1898 self-portrait, when he used battery-powered arc lamps to light the murky depths. Rightfully heralded as "the father of the underwater camera," Boutan was aware that he had merely taken the first steps in an enormous marine adventure that knew no bounds. "I have opened the way," he wrote, urging others to follow him in recording the limitless saga of the sea.

It is unlikely that even the visionary Boutan could have imagined that eighty-nine years later, camera equipment would be so reliable and so sophisticated that scientists could photograph in eerie detail the grave of the "unsinkable" *Titanic*, clearly capturing on film one of its elegant crystal chandeliers, still intact and still swaying gracefully to the beat of restless marine currents on the floor of the North Atlantic.

Explored by adventurous underwater scientists such as France's Jacques-Yves Cousteau and Canada's Joe MacInnis, the oceans are slowly, if reluctantly, yielding up their secrets, giving us access to vital information about what Cousteau has so graphically described as "our planet's lifebelt." In honor of the pioneering Professor Boutan, Captain Cousteau christened his first research vessel the *Boutan*.

One of the vital tools in the ongoing adventure of oceanic exploration has been the underwater camera that curious marine biologists and divers have taken with them into the waters of the world's mysterious oceans.

1898
UNDERWATER SELF-PORTRAIT

LOUIS BOUTAN / FRENCH 1859–1934

14

Lewis Hine was born in Oshkosh, Wisconsin, in 1874. As a young boy, he worked long hours in a local factory, experiencing at first hand conditions he would later document so vividly with his camera.

In 1903, he acquired a camera and a flashgun, and within a few years became one of the foremost investigative reporters of his day. He first examined the lives of some of the hundreds of thousands of immigrant families who were then crowding the customs sheds at Ellis Island. What happened to them once they set foot on the promised land? His photographs showed the appalling conditions that awaited most immigrants: overcrowded, filthy slums; violent, dangerous streets; and poor-paying, enslaving jobs at which men and women toiled to support their young families.

Next he turned the illuminating light of his camera on the horrific conditions in America's coal mines. He recorded the squalor and desperation suffered by miners and their families. Even the government was shocked by photographs of boys – often as young as nine or ten years of age – dirty-faced, pale, undernourished, employed as breaker boys in the unhealthy and dangerous interiors of the nation's coal mines.

Hine soon earned the sobriquet that was to stick with him until the end of his days: "the conscience with a camera." In 1908, he was hired as a photographer by the federal government's National Child Labor Committee to investigate child labor conditions in the United States. Hine's pictures of children, ill clothed and barefoot, tending machines in Carolina cotton mills, stunned America. Hine realized only too clearly that these ragged, exploited children, who had no chance for an education or hope for the future, were not the only victims. By employing a massive child labor force (over forty thousand children under sixteen years of age worked in cotton mills), industry was also enslaving an entire adult labor force, undercut by this cheap child labor.

Hine's photographs were published widely in newspapers, magazines, and National Child Labor Committee reports, and he used them in illustrated lectures decrying the terrible plight of America's working children. What dry statistics and long-winded reports could not accomplish, Hine's photographs did. Many believe that as a direct result of the publication of photographs as disturbing as this vulnerable little girl working in a cotton mill, the federal government introduced legislation to put an end to such child labor practices.

Reformers such as Lewis Hine, and others who joined him in his lifelong crusade against social injustice, perceived their cause as a "holy war" and they battled like warriors to end the terrible economic exploitation of children.

1909
CHILD SPINNER, NORTH CAROLINA

LEWIS W. HINE / AMERICAN 1874–1940

15

Even from behind, he may have been the most recognized figure in the world. Recognized, that is, not as himself, but as the Little Tramp, a character he created for himself in 1914 and which today still has the power to evoke laughter and tears from adoring fans on every continent of the globe.

Charlie Chaplin mastered the art of pantomime and slapstick as no other actor has ever done. Sporting an ill-fitting frock coat, baggy pants, bowler hat, and oversized shoes, he strutted across the screen carrying a pliable bamboo cane that seemed to have a mischievous mind of its own. Chaplin became the first Hollywood star to win an international reputation; his characters became the stuff of folklore and legends. Young children giggled as they sang:

> Charlie Chaplin went to France
> To teach the ladies how to dance.

Or, to the tune of "Gentle Jesus":

> Charlie Chaplin meek and mild
> Took a sausage from a child.
> When the child began to cry
> Charlie slapped him in the eye.

George Bernard Shaw, H. G. Wells, Albert Einstein, and Winston Churchill were among his enthusiastic and admiring fans. In his lifetime he made some 225 films, most of which, incredibly, he wrote and directed himself.

Chaplin's photograph, depicting the tenderhearted Little Tramp, is perhaps the most famous motion picture "still" in the history of the movies. He symbolized the little man's perpetual struggle against the system, and he won hearts all over the world with his portrayal of one man's (often ludicrous) attempts to change the way things are. With his antic escapades and his comic genius, he succeeded in turning a rather sad old world, briefly, into a very funny place. And for that great gift of laughter he has earned countless critics' acclaim as the greatest theatrical artist of all time.

1914
CHARLIE CHAPLIN

MOTION PICTURE STILL

16

Afterward they called him "Lucky Lindy," but when twenty-five-year-old Captain Charles A. Lindbergh lifted off from Roosevelt Field, Long Island, on the world's first solo flight across the brooding Atlantic Ocean, few were there to wish him well. For sustenance during the thirty-six-hundred-mile flight from New York to Paris, he had packed five sandwiches, two canteens of water, and some emergency army rations. His fragile monoplane carried 451 gallons of gasoline and the hopes and fears of a young man who believed in his own ability and flying skills to navigate successfully the great-circle route – the shortest route – between the continents.

When he touched down in Paris thirty-three hours and thirty minutes later, his first words were, "Well, I made it." News of his safe arrival was flashed around the world, and people shouted to one another in the streets of America, "Lindbergh is in Paris!" Some detractors, irritated by the near mass hysteria that greeted his accomplishment, claimed he had been spurred on to the dangerous flight by avarice: the twenty-five thousand dollars' prize money put up by Manhattan hotel owner Raymond Orteig for the world's first solo, nonstop flight from New York to Paris.

But the flight of the *Spirit of St. Louis* was about more than one man's quest for the pot of gold at the end of the rainbow. Lindbergh's feat symbolized the spirit of an age that celebrated man's unquenchable drive to be free and to dream impossible dreams. His victory was perceived by millions as a great triumph of the individual will, and his courage and daring inspired an age hungry for heroes. He had conquered the skies and captivated the imagination of the world.

For those who could not be in Paris to witness the arrival of Lindbergh's heroic transatlantic flight, this photograph of a daring young man and his tiny plane brought home the magic and excitement of the moment.

1927
CHARLES LINDBERGH AND THE *SPIRIT OF ST. LOUIS*, PARIS

PHOTOGRAPHER UNKNOWN

17

Garbo – no one ever called her Greta, a name she hated – was one of Hollywood's legendary movie stars. She projected a new ideal of feminine beauty, inspiring many to refer to her with rapturous adulation as "the Divine Garbo."

She was the creation not of the media, not even of her movies (she was never considered a truly great actress), but of the man who photographed her from the start of her career until the day she forsook Hollywood forever – Clarence Sinclair Bull. The photographs Bull made of Garbo were the final, sublime achievement of the perfection early photographers struggled for in their smelly laboratories. She was a "drawing made with light" – the definitive, perfect "heliograph."

Bull used studio lighting with a skill that has rarely been equaled. He employed it as a science and as an art. With a key light here and a top light there, he accented her lovely features, her aloof beauty, her hint of mystery, her beguiling allure. With lights and shadows, he created a near perfect face – a face many believe more beautiful than the *Mona Lisa*. In the darkroom he would call upon all his superb printing and retouching skills to produce the golden-toned image the world would embrace as the incomparable Garbo.

Clarence Bull wielded the painless scalpel of light to correct facial flaws and imperfections that are today almost exclusively the domain of the plastic surgeon. And he was only one of a brilliant and talented team of men and women who came to be known as the great Hollywood portrait photographers, among them George Hurrell, Laszlo Willinger, Joseph von Sternberg, and Ruth Harriet Louise. Together they invented a new school of publicity photography that was instantly recognizable. With their versatile large-format cameras, they immortalized the stars: Joan Crawford, Carole Lombard, Marlene Dietrich, not to mention the male heartthrobs, Clark Gable, Cary Grant, Gary Cooper. With the flick of a light they made the stars look sexy, sad, or sullen. And they could erase faults in an actor's face quicker than pressing a button on a computer to eliminate unwanted information.

Hollywood's great portrait photographers didn't merely photograph the stars; they created the stars. They didn't merely capture an actor's image; they invented the image. And in the process they produced some of the finest, most sought-after photographs in the world. They defined glamor and gave it to the kings and queens of the silver screen, those beautiful people who will always be remembered as forever young, forever desirable.

1930
GRETA GARBO

CLARENCE SINCLAIR BULL / AMERICAN 1895–1979

18

Harold Edgerton is generally regarded as the scientist who, while he did not invent strobe lighting, perfected the equipment so that clear, sharp pictures could be made with exposures as brief as one-millionth of a second. When his photograph of a drop of milk falling onto a red plate was published in 1931 it created a sensation with an incredulous and enchanted public.

In fact, the first photograph of a splash of milk had been made some thirty years earlier. It was an experiment by A. M. Worthington, who used magnesia terminals to provide the requisite illumination for his stop-action photograph. The image, indistinct and rather nondescript, attracted scant attention. It was left to the energetic Dr. Edgerton to produce the photographs of breathtaking loveliness that are regarded now as works of art.

In 1931, Edgerton was a researcher at the Massachusetts Institute of Technology (where he still conducts his experiments today) when he devised a new technique using high-intensity stroboscopic lighting. This powerful new aid to observation revealed a realm of visual surprises. The invisible world had been made visible in a way never before experienced.

Scientists have been probing beyond the limits of the human eye for centuries, but when they began employing photographic techniques as an instrument in their research, the results often startled and frightened their fellow men. When Wilhelm Conrad Roentgen discovered X rays in 1895, the world was astonished to see skeletons, generally associated only with the dead, lurking ghostlike inside living bodies.

High-speed photography and multiple exposures had, of course, been around for a long time. The celebrated French artist Marcel Duchamp credited multiple-exposure photographs with giving him the creative stimulus to paint his world-famous painting *Nude Descending a Staircase*. The influence of photography on the early Impressionists is well documented. The interesting development that Edgerton's photographs fostered was the increasing frequency with which scientific photographs were exhibited as aesthetic productions. The inherent beauty revealed in his images created enormous interest, and the public clamored to buy them. Ansel Adams, the revered American photographer, was extravagant in his praise of Edgerton's photographs.

Today high-powered cameras using the latest electronic support systems are probing the mysteries of the cosmos and capturing pictures of our hidden universe. In the case of the photographs of Saturn taken by the spaceship *Voyager 1* from five million miles away, scientists obtained more information about Saturn than had been discovered in the 370 years since Galileo first trained his telescope on the distant planet. The photographs indeed represented an amazingly detailed scientific record, but to many who marveled at the extraordinary splendor of Saturn and its rings, objects of shimmering and glorious beauty, they looked suspiciously like art.

The Light Gallery in New York appeared to support this position when it presented an exhibition of NASA photographs in conjunction with work by Ansel Adams. Reviving the old debate, one critic, Gene Thornton, chose to repudiate the NASA photographs as not worthy of the distinction. "One of the supreme photographic achievements of modern times, yes," he opined, "but art, no."

The academic squabble was lost on most wide-eyed beholders who would never again gaze upon the heavenly planets, or upon photographs of them, with quite the same degree of cool or unfeeling detachment.

1931
DROP OF MILK

HAROLD E. EDGERTON / AMERICAN 1903–

19

Walker Evans once said, "Photography is about pleasure and photography is about pain." There can be no doubt, once one looks into the faces of this impoverished family of a tenant farmer in Hale County, Alabama, that this photograph is about pain.

In 1935, Evans joined the Farm Security Administration, one of a myriad of new government agencies established by President Franklin D. Roosevelt to help relieve the terrible grip of the Depression on the one-third of America he described as "ill-housed, ill-clothed, and ill-fed." Evans was a master of the photographic style that was labeled documentary. With his clear, penetrating vision, he recorded directly and without artifice what he perceived to be the photographic facts.

In 1941, Evans collaborated with writer James Agee on a book, *Let Us Now Praise Famous Men*, a moving study of tenant farmers in America. Compelling and compassionate, it took an unblinking look at rural poverty, one of the worst blights of American society. The book's influence was immense. Critics praised Evans for his sensibility, claiming that he had found poetry and meaning where lesser photographers might have found only poverty and ugliness. But Evans' documentary photographs were intended to do much more than convey information. His aim was to persuade and to convince and to effect change.

In these and other photographs made during his tenure with the Farm Security Administration, Evans looked inside the sorrowing heart of America. He once confided to a friend, "I guess I'm deeply in love with America," and he expressed his love by focusing on the desperate need for public assistance to ease the plight of America's beleaguered farmers and their destitute families. Prompted in part by the reality of Evans' photographs, the assistance came.

SHARECROPP

WALKER EVANS

ely simple operation. Modern tech-
t are constantly reducing the possi-
calculation. But to make a great
by. The renowned American photog-
Photography is knowing where to
complex process. A dozen questions
photographer. And until that crucial
he final decision and releases the
possibilities intrude upon the mind.
otographs with amazing consistency
was part of a small but astonishingly
l for the legendary Roy E. Stryker,
tion's photographic project. Their
hat existed in rural America were
es across the country in an effort to
programs to assist the rural poor
The photograph "Migrant Mother"
y Stryker's group and is one of the
ographs in history.
n and a talented artist. She consis-
ividuals trapped by forces beyond
usted mother with her three small
up in Nipomo, California. Lange's
ea field where the crop had failed in
he car to buy food. She was thirty-

especially this photograph, made a
Steinbeck, author of the influential
d the subsequent film based on it,
rant workers and forced those in
e working conditions.
graph has survived its initial jour-
f a cry for help. It is admired today
time cannot diminish.

1936
MIGRANT MOTHER

DOROTHEA LANGE / AMERICAN 1895–1965

21

This photograph of Jesse Owens, flashed over the news wires in the spring of 1936, recorded the event that shattered Hitler's hopes for the Berlin Olympic Games and the Nazi myth of Aryan superiority. The twenty-two-year-old black American was born, the grandson of slaves, in the cotton-growing community of Danville, Alabama. Growing up poor, Jesse Owens began to run at the age of nine. "We had nothing to do but run. We couldn't afford any kind of equipment, so we ran and ran and ran."

And run he did until he came to be known as the greatest runner of his time. At the 1936 Berlin Olympics he captured four gold medals, turning in record-shattering performances in the two-hundred-meter race and the broad jump, tying the world record in the hundred-meter race, and anchoring the victorious U.S. four-hundred-meter relay team.

It was generally believed at the time that an angry Hitler had snubbed Owens by leaving the stadium without congratulating him. The American press was quick to exploit the incident, adding fuel to the fierce nationalism of the thirties. But, in fact, there was no such snub. Hitler, who had jumped into the limelight to pose shaking hands with the first day's winners, was quickly informed by the Belgian head of the International Olympic Committee, Count Henri de Baillet-Latour, that it was not his role and he would henceforth refrain from congratulating the medalists. From that day on, Hitler did not congratulate any of the winners.

Unfortunately, as Owens remembered shortly before his death in 1980, "After all the stories about Hitler and his snub, I came back to my native country and I couldn't ride in the front of the bus. I wasn't invited up to shake hands with Hitler – but I wasn't invited to the White House to shake hands with the President either." Nevertheless, Jesse Owens and that other great black champion of the day, Joe Louis, became heroes to the youth of the nation, and especially to the black youth of America.

In 1976, Jesse Owens received a little of the glory and recognition long due an outstanding athlete. President Gerald Ford presented him with the Presidential Medal of Freedom at the White House on August 5, 1976. And in February 1979, President Jimmy Carter presented him with the Living Legends Award, noting that since Owens' "superb achievement, he has continued in his own dedicated but modest way to inspire others to reach for greatness."

Jesse Owens left his mark on the athletes and youth of America. He lived to see his great Olympic feat inspire thousands more who ran in his triumphant footsteps.

1936
JESSE OWENS, OLYMPIC GAMES, BERLIN

PHOTOGRAPHER UNKNOWN

22

He has been called the greatest combat photographer of all time. In his brief forty-one-year life, Robert Capa covered five wars, always adhering to his own strict advice to fellow photographers: "If your pictures aren't good enough, you aren't close enough."

Handsome and debonair, dashing and glamorous, Capa was also a consummate professional renowned for his coolness and bravery under fire. In the fall of 1936 Capa, a passionate anti-fascist who championed the cause of the Spanish Loyalist government in its bitter civil war against the right-wing Nationalist army of General Francisco Franco, was covering the fighting near Cerro Muriano on the Córdoba front when he made this photograph. It was published in France on September 23, 1936, with the caption "Death of a Loyalist Soldier." *Life* magazine ran it the following year. Since then it has been published countless times and is recognized as perhaps the most famous war photograph ever taken.

Almost forty years later a British journalist claimed that the picture had been contrived. Capa's biographer, Richard Whelan, discounted the rumor and offered compelling arguments to support the authenticity of Capa's photograph: ". . . it seems rather improbable that a soldier would have agreed to stage a photograph that purported to show his own death. (For one thing, soldiers tend to be very superstitious about such matters.) If it had been a question of international fakery, it seems more likely that all involved would have preferred to stage pictures of victory. But in the end, after all the controversy and speculation, the fact remains that Capa's [photograph] is a great and powerful image, a haunting symbol of all the Loyalist soldiers who died in the war, and of Republican Spain itself, flinging itself bravely forward and being struck down."

Capa's own words, reported in the New York *World Telegram*, should be remembered as well: "No tricks are necessary to take pictures in Spain. . . . The pictures are there, and you just take them. The truth is the best picture, the best propaganda."

Capa was killed in 1954 while covering the French war against Ho Chi Minh in Indochina. Pressing ahead of the French troops to photograph the marching men, he ran across a field and was mortally wounded by an exploding land mine. When his companions reached him moments later, they comforted the dying Capa, who still cradled his precious camera in his left hand.

For many who recognize and remember this picture from reproductions in magazines and newspapers, it remains a vivid symbol of the terrible violence of war and the painful, unutterable agony of the moment of death. Today, more than half a century later, Robert Capa's "Death of a Loyalist Soldier" retains all of its power to convey the brutality and banality of armed conflict. "War is hell" exhibited its grimmest, most graphic reality in Capa's photographs from the combat zone.

Edward Steichen, founding director of the Museum of Modern Art's photography department, paid Capa a dazzling tribute: "Robert Capa knew and hated war. In his vivid, factual photographs he recorded its horror and monstrous stupidity with the same fervor and passion revealed in Goya's famous etchings, 'The Disasters of War'. . .he lived his life valiantly and vigorously and with rare integrity." No photographer could wish for a better epitaph and no photographer has ever received a finer one.

1936
DEATH OF A LOYALIST SOLDIER

ROBERT CAPA / AMERICAN 1913–1954

23

It was market day in the Spanish town of Guernica, and most of the inhabitants were gathered in the main square of the small Basque city. The bitter civil war had been raging for almost a year between the Republican government and the Nationalist forces led by General Franco. Hitler and Mussolini, fearing that a Communist Spain would threaten their plans for a fascist Europe, threw their military might on the side of the Nationalists.

On April 26, 1937, at 4:40 P.M., the Condor Legion, pride of Hermann Goering's fledgling Luftwaffe, bombed peaceful, undefended Guernica to virtually total destruction. It took three hours and five minutes. For the German high command, it was an opportunity for their fighter pilots to practice saturation-bombing and dive-bombing techniques designed to terrorize and kill fleeing civilians.

Photographers and journalists who reported the bombing described it as an atrocity of then unparalleled horror. Guernica was the first city in history to be destroyed by aerial bombardment. World War II, for which the Spanish Civil War was a military dress rehearsal, would ultimately numb the world with its terrible devastation of Dresden and Hiroshima. While a complacent world was loathe to challenge the denials of Franco, the Germans, and the Vatican, one man decided to reveal the dimensions of the atrocity.

Photographs of the Basque bombing appeared in Paris newspapers within a day or two. And Pablo Picasso, acclaimed by many as the artistic genius of our age, immediately began his preliminary sketches for the mural *Guernica*, which he gave to the Republican government to hang in the 1937 International Exposition in Paris. Today, *Guernica* is widely hailed as the greatest political painting of the twentieth century.

Much controversy has arisen as to the specific meaning of the various elements of the painting. Does the bull represent fascism? Spain? Brutality and darkness? Picasso himself, never one to be bound by other people's need for precise references, was no help. Critics have had a field day dissecting and explaining the masterpiece. What has never been in doubt is that the powerful mural is a symbolic, allegorical painting made to express an exiled Spaniard's terrible rage at the agony imposed on a defenseless town of innocent men, women, and children. He was painting their agony, Spain's agony, and his own agony.

A few years later, when German soldiers visited Picasso's studio in Paris during the occupation of France in World War II, the painter handed out postcards of the *Guernica* mural to his unwanted and uninvited visitors.

"Did you do this?" one of the surprised soldiers exclaimed.

"No," Picasso is reputed to have replied, "you did."

1937
THE BOMBING OF GUERNICA, SPAIN

PHOTOGRAPHER UNKNOWN

24

This endearing photograph of President Franklin Delano Roosevelt – FDR, as he was familiarly known – was made by an unknown photographer in 1939. Roosevelt had won the presidency in 1932, when America was reeling from the devastating economic woes of the Depression triggered by the stock market crash of October 1929.

Nine million Americans were out of work; 40 percent of the nation's families had annual incomes well below a thousand dollars. "My friends," the confident new president assured the people in his inaugural address, "the only thing we have to fear is fear itself."

For a despairing country, he initiated a bold New Deal and quickly created a rash of federally financed agencies to reorganize agriculture and industry. He was attacked in the press, criticized as a socialist out to give the country away. But the Work Projects Administration alone funneled billions of dollars directly into millions of needy households. A quarter of a million miles of roads were constructed and one thousand airports repaired or built. By 1936, he had roused a nation to action with his ringing oratory: "This generation has a rendezvous with Destiny!"

Franklin Delano Roosevelt was one of those individuals whom the camera "loved." His jaunty smile and the cocky tilt of his chin inspired warmth and trust wherever he appeared across the nation. He guided the country through the dangerous shoals of a terrible economic crisis, and when the war came, as he recognized it would, he galvanized an isolationist, anti-war nation into a state of readiness. When the Japanese struck their treacherous blow at Pearl Harbor, it was Roosevelt who led a united nation into World War II. In 1944, he won an unprecedented fourth term as president and commander in chief.

Roosevelt died on April 12, 1945, from a cerebral hemorrhage. He was mourned across the country; many wept openly when his funeral cortege passed.

For the great multitude of Americans who had sat close to their radio sets to listen with rapt attention to Roosevelt's popular fireside chats, the image of the president they carried in their hearts and minds most closely resembled this photograph of a beloved leader who personified hope and confidence.

1939
FRANKLIN DELANO ROOSEVELT

PHOTOGRAPHER UNKNOWN

1968
EXECUTION OF A VIET CONG SUSPECT, SAIGON

EDDIE ADAMS / AMERICAN 1933–

THIS SCENE IS THE BASIS FOR THE
ISLEY BRO. SONG "FOUR DEAD IN OHIO"

Public protest against the long and costly war in Vietnam was becoming increasingly vociferous by the spring of 1970. Anti-war rallies and marches were a fact of life at university campuses across America. On April 30, 1970, President Richard Nixon appeared on national television to announce another escalation in the hostilities. Recent military intelligence reports had indicated that large numbers of Viet Cong were finding refuge and a base for their operations in nearby Cambodia. Therefore, a major American-South Vietnamese offensive into Cambodia was to be launched. The anti-war movement responded with more protest demonstrations.

At Ohio's Kent State University, the atmosphere was particularly tense. There, angry students had hurled rocks and flares at an ROTC building, starting a fire that caused extensive damage. The governor of Ohio hurriedly ordered nine hundred national guardsmen to the area "to restore order." A state of emergency was declared and demonstrations were banned.

On Monday, May 4, more than a thousand students assembled to confront the soldiers. Most assumed the guardsmen carried blanks in their rifles; in fact, they had come with loaded guns. The demonstrators advanced toward the guardsmen, who had formed two lines facing the protesters. Suddenly and without warning, the soldiers opened fire.

Subsequent investigations failed to reveal who gave the order to fire, or why. The tragic consequences were denounced worldwide. Four young students were killed, one of them the girl who earlier had slipped a flower into the barrel of a guardsman's rifle with the wistful comment, "Flowers are better than bullets."

This photograph of an anguished young woman shouting her rage over the dead body of a fellow student sent a frightful message to Washington. The war had come to America itself.

The picture's remarkable power and immediacy won a Pulitzer Prize for the young student photographer who snapped photos as he ran toward the bloody scene. Today it is one of the most vividly remembered photographs of the Vietnam protest movement.

1970
SHOOTING AT KENT STATE UNIVERSITY, OHIO

JOHN FILO / AMERICAN 1948–

When the Canadian writer-philosopher Marshall McLuhan wrote, "The war in Vietnam was lost in the living rooms of the nation," he may have had this horrifying image in mind. The fact that these pitifully burned South Vietnamese children had been wounded by the fiery jelly of napalm dropped in error by a South Vietnamese Skyraider adds immeasurably to the pain of this agonizing photograph. The silent screams of the tormented victims will haunt America's conscience for years to come.

The incident took place twenty-five miles northwest of Saigon, near the marketplace of Trangbang. North Vietnamese troops had blockaded the road running from the capital at Saigon to the Cambodian border. The battleground was a military deadlock, and the South Vietnamese officers called for an air strike.

South Vietnamese soldiers watched in horror as one of the attacking planes mistakenly dropped its load of flaming napalm on their own troops and on civilians. Several children, severely burned, fled down the road screaming. Nine-year-old Phan Thi Kim Phuc, in the center of the photograph, tore off her burning clothes as she ran.

Miraculously, the little girl, although badly burned, survived. She was dubbed the "napalm girl" by the media, and press dispatches frequently reported on her medical recovery. Most recently, she was described as still suffering from searing headaches and periodic throbbing pain.

With this never-to-be-forgotten photograph, America's longest, most unpopular war was dealt a crushing blow.

1972
SOUTH VIETNAMESE CHILDREN BURNED BY NAPALM

NICK (HUYNH CONG) UT / AMERICAN 1951–

Through five decades, *Life* magazine published the work of dozens of extraordinarily talented photographers. Every week millions of readers observed the world through the eyes of these sensitive men and women who roamed the planet with their cameras, capturing hitherto unseen aspects of life on earth.

Eugene Smith was one of these – the photographer who, some say, perfected the photo-story technique. In 1972, he was sent to Japan by *Life* to produce a photographic essay on the mercury pollution at Minamata.

The Chisso Corporation had been officially charged by the Japanese government with having caused widespread birth defects and environmental pollution through its careless discharge of methyl mercury. Officially, 181 victims were identified as "Minamata disease" patients, but many hundreds of people living in the towns and countryside surrounding the industrial plant were consuming contaminated fish and accumulating methyl mercury in their bodies. The guilt of the Chisso Corporation was never in doubt. What was debated was the extent of the crime and the amount of compensation due to the victims and their families.

This photograph of a Japanese mother tenderly bathing her seventeen-year-old daughter, deformed since birth as a result of mercury poisoning, became a symbol of the cost in human suffering and a warning to others to halt the wanton destruction of the earth by industrial waste. The shot was published by *Life* and by newspapers and magazines worldwide. It aroused an international rallying cry: curb the ravages of industrial pollution and make the polluters pay.

More eloquent than the strident voices or clenched fists of angry protesters, Smith's photograph demonstrated a moving compassion for Minamata's victims and for those who minister to them. It affirmed the fundamental value of human life and the need to place people above the reckless pursuit of industrial progress.

1972
TOMOKO IN HER BATH, JAPAN

W. EUGENE SMITH / AMERICAN 1918–1978

In the end it was Terry Fox himself who was the miracle. His story did not in the beginning seem unusual, and his heroic exploit did not at first attract much notice. He had lost his right leg to cancer and was determined to focus public attention on the need for more funds to support cancer research. His strategy was simple and ingenuous. He would run across Canada on his good left leg and an artificial limb, undertaking a five-thousand-mile "Marathon of Hope" to demonstrate to others disabled by cancer that the loss of a limb was an obstacle that could be overcome.

On April 12, 1980, he dipped his artificial leg into the frigid Atlantic Ocean at St. John's, Newfoundland. Terry began his odyssey with high hopes and good humor, despite scant media attention. Soon enthusiasm grew for the spunky youth, and funds that were collected along the route began to mount.

In 144 days he traveled an incredible 3,339 miles, uphill and downhill, through biting cold, incessant rain, and – when spring moved into summer – staggering heat. He wore out one artificial limb after another, and he ran in almost constant pain on an amputated stump that was bleeding and covered with sores.

On Monday, September 1, Terry was up at 4 A.M. and on the road at 5 A.M. He ran an exhausting twenty-two miles before he collapsed with the fearful words, "Take me to a hospital." X rays revealed that the virulent cancer had spread to both lungs. Terry had been running with one lung collapsed, the other filling with fluid. His condition was beyond treatment. At home in Port Coquitlam, British Columbia, Terry Fox died on June 28, 1981. He was twenty-two.

Weeks before his death, a grieving nation had bestowed on him the highest honor his country could give: Companion of the Order of Canada. He would be remembered as a handsome young man with an endearing smile who had run across the rugged terrain of six provinces before a cruel fate dashed his hopes.

As it happened, it was not the distance covered that really mattered. Terry Fox accomplished what he set out to do. A young man with a dream had captured the heart of every Canadian and millions more around the world who had followed his journey with admiration and support. Donations poured in from the United States, Great Britain, Europe, and Japan. To date, over seventy million dollars has been raised in his name for cancer research.

Nations and peoples have been divided politically, culturally, linguistically, and in myriad other ways throughout history. The triumph of Terry Fox may have been that he was one of the few human beings to unite an entire nation in love and admiration and common purpose.

This photograph of an anguished but determined young man struggling against an implacable fate is above all a portrait of courage.

1980
TERRY FOX

GAIL HARVEY / CANADIAN 1952–

Less than sixty-six years after the Wright brothers coaxed their fragile craft off the ground at Kitty Hawk, North Carolina, on December 17, 1903, American astronauts Neil Armstrong and Edwin Aldrin walked and danced on the moon.

Orville Wright, assisted by his brother, Wilbur, flew a distance of 120 feet in twelve seconds. The astronauts were 239,000 miles from home. Their journey took four days, six hours, and forty-five minutes. In cold hard cash, the epic-making moon walk cost some twenty-five billion dollars. In human effort and sacrifice, the cost was not measurable. But on July 20, 1969, at 4:17 P.M. EDT, a dream that has fired man's imagination from the dawn of time was fulfilled. "Tranquility Base here. The *Eagle* has landed."

It was the camera that brought it all home. As Neil Armstrong made the first footprint on the powdery surface of the lunar landscape, an image was etched forever in the memory of the world. The photograph, relayed with remarkable clarity to enthralled audiences all over the globe, was to become as famous as his oft quoted first words: "That's one small step for a man, one giant leap for mankind."

After twenty-one and a half hours that included exploration and photography sessions, the *Apollo 11* astronauts prepared to cast off from the moon for their space voyage back to planet earth. As well as their footprints and the American flag, they left behind a plaque proclaiming, "We came in peace for all mankind."

There were some members of the Flat Earth Society who insisted, for whatever mischievous or cantankerous reasons of their own, that it was all a hoax. But for a wondering, watching world, the picture of two exuberant men cavorting on the distant surface of the moon was a thrilling, miraculous accomplishment. On that historic day, even the most timorous of earthlings was inspired to believe in man's ability to reach the stars.

1969
EDWIN "BUZZ" ALDRIN ON THE MOON

NEIL ARMSTRONG / AMERICAN 1930–

In the late seventies photographs of baby harp seals were everywhere. Newspapers and magazines gave them front-page treatment. Protesters sported buttons emblazoned with the irresistible face of a young pup. The images unleashed a groundswell of emotion and an equally powerful flood of angry letters.

From the start the battle over the seal hunt was an uneven contest. Children, animal lovers, and countless others who had never before publicly espoused a cause found themselves passionately concerned about the fate of tens of thousands of baby harp seals killed annually for their valuable white pelts. They hastened to sign petitions urging the Canadian government to "stop the slaughter."

For troubled conservationists, the effort to save the seals became a personal crusade. French film star Brigitte Bardot joined the growing army of protesters and was photographed on an ice floe cradling a baby seal in her arms. Lurid photographs and newsreel footage of sealers crushing the skulls of seal pups and skinning them while the animals appeared to be still alive aroused worldwide indignation.

Government scientists and politicians published statistics and charts in an attempt to prove that the seal herds were not endangered and that the baby seals were dead when their pelts were removed. But against the raw emotional impact of photographs such as this one, dry government reports had little influence. In 1983, the European Economic Community, previously a major customer for the luxurious white fur pelts, voted to ban the import of seal skins. Status-conscious women in many countries got the message, some refusing to wear any sort of fur at all.

The seal hunters, men from Newfoundland and the Magdalen Islands in the Gulf of St. Lawrence, were, not unexpectedly, bitter and dismayed. They claimed that the seal hunt had played an important role in their modest economic life for generations, and they found allies in the cod fishermen of the area, who warned that unrestricted seal herds would in time devastate the cod fishery. The fishermen mounted a flamboyant campaign of their own: "Save our cod, eat a seal."

Determined Greenpeace activists, with the support of the International Fund for Animal Welfare, continued to interfere with the hunt, spraying baby seals with a harmless but permanent red or green dye that rendered the pelts valueless. The hunters were left to ponder their international image as cruel and indifferent murderers of defenseless seal pups. What, they wanted to know, was the difference between killing a seal for his pelt and a pig for his bacon?

In 1984, a royal commission was given the responsibility of investigating the sealing industry in Canada. It found that the commercial hunting of seal pups was "unacceptable" to the public and therefore should not be permitted. In 1987, the hunting of baby harp seals was officially ended, and a new industry was born. Come springtime each year, eager tourists are flown to the Gulf of St. Lawrence, where they marvel at the spectacle of thousands of newborn seals frolicking on the pack ice.

1977
HARP SEAL PUP

FRED BRUEMMER / CANADIAN 1929–

The image has stamped itself permanently on the visual memory of the world. It seemed all the more horrific because, as the unthinkable happened, it traced a pattern of terrible beauty. Smoky white tendrils etched an unforgettable picture against a clear blue sky.

In hindsight, the *Challenger* explosion was a catastrophe waiting to happen. On January 28, 1986, the mighty spaceship – laden with the utmost in electronic wizardry, six astronauts, and a delighted schoolteacher – lifted majestically off the ground. Thousands of excited schoolchildren waited anxiously for their first science lesson from space. Seventy-three seconds after blast-off, the pride of America's vaunted space program was consumed in an awesome fireball. The image was relayed around the globe almost instantaneously by satellite communication. The watching world gasped in disbelief.

America's celebrated space program, begun in jubilant expectation twenty-five years earlier – when President Kennedy had prophesied, accurately as it turned out, that American technology would land a man on the moon within a decade – was now indefinitely grounded pending a full and vigorous investigation. The inquiry would stir up a blizzard of problems and questions. In particular, it would focus on how a multi-billion-dollar shuttlecraft, popularly perceived to be an electronic marvel, could be sent aloft with a faulty synthetic rubber O-ring designed to prevent superhot gases from escaping and igniting the ship's liquid fuel tank.

The tragedy of the disaster became even more unbearable as investigators revealed that NASA had been repeatedly warned that the reliability of the O-rings was marginal. If not corrected, their weakness could lead to "catastrophic failure." Not only did America have to deal with the horror of the explosion and the loss of seven brave citizens, but it had to absorb the painful knowledge that it had sent innocent people to their deaths in a machine that had been described as having faulty parts and equipment. America had put its best and its brightest at unconscionable risk. America had placed its faith in the god of technology, and the god had betrayed that faith.

Government officials would attempt to erase the nightmare picture from America's troubled memory. Accidents will happen. Tragedy is the price of progress. But the moment was burned into the conscience of a nation with a vividness and a clarity that nothing could erase. The picture of the *Challenger* explosion was a part of the shared pain that bound a sorrowing nation together in grief and remembrance.

1986

THE *CHALLENGER* EXPLODES

NASA

This photograph of a colossal, majestic woman holding a torch aloft could be flashed on every television screen in the world, printed on the front page of every newspaper and magazine in the world, mailed as a souvenir postcard to anywhere in the world – and just about anyone who saw the image would immediately recognize it as the most famous monument in the world: the Statue of Liberty.

She is the creation of the French artist and sculptor Frédéric Auguste Bartholdi, who in 1865 first conceived the idea of a gigantic sculpture to symbolize the friendship between France and America. Twenty-one years later, on a foggy October day in 1886, the enormous structure was unveiled before a gala crowd of onlookers. Thousands watched from shore while others cheered from a flotilla of steamers, ferryboats, and yachts that bobbed in the harbor.

Bartholdi, who was present, confidently predicted that "this statue will exist thousands of years from now, long after our names have been forgotten." But even Bartholdi, in his artist's pride and enthusiasm, could not have predicted the incredible influence that the lady would have on the imagination of the world. She has become a symbol for what America is all about – the land of opportunity and the land of the free.

She stands a commanding 305^1/$_2$ feet tall above her enormous pedestal on Liberty Island. Over twelve million immigrants sailed past the beckoning statue in the heyday of American immigration. Today their descendants number over one hundred million, many of whom still remember her with fond affection.

Legend has it that Bartholdi used his mother as his inspiration for the serenely beautiful face of the statue. In classical garb, she holds a tablet in her left hand with the date of the Declaration of Independence inscribed upon it. In her right hand she holds high a torch, originally conceived by the artist as a symbol of enlightenment, but to every American the torch of freedom.

Through the years she has become much more than a gesture of France's admiration of and affinity for the ideals that inspired the American War of Independence. She has become a uniquely American institution and symbol. There is a foundation to preserve her heritage, to oversee her recent mammoth restoration, and to protect her as the most beloved of America's public treasures.

Everyone calls her "the lady" – presidents, politicians, and the American public, which honors her second only to the American flag. In World War I, men of the 77th Liberty Division fought in helmets emblazoned with her insignia, and in one dramatic burst of patriotic fervor, eighteen thousand officers and men at Camp Dodge in Des Moines, Iowa, formed themselves into a living replica of the statue as a jaunty salute to their favorite "all-American girl." And, of course, she has been exploited by American entrepreneurs to sell everything from deodorants to tobacco, from matches to soap.

Closely associated with the Statue of Liberty will always be the words written in 1883 by New York poet Emma Lazarus. A bronze tablet commemorating the completion of the pedestal in 1903 has the lines of Emma's poem engraved in it. Most people would not recognize all of the fourteen-line verse, but almost everyone can quote the now immortal last lines:

> Give me your tired, your poor,
> Your huddled masses yearning to breathe free,
> The wretched refuse of your teeming shore,
> Send these, the homeless, tempest-tost to me,
> I lift my lamp beside the golden door!

1980
THE STATUE OF LIBERTY

ARAM GESAR / AMERICAN

From the beginning of time, mankind has had a rapturous fascination with the spectacle provided by sunrises and sunsets. Painters have painted them. Poets have serenaded them. Heaven knows, since the invention of the camera, photographers have photographed them.

The beloved French writer and aviator Antoine de Saint-Exupéry told of a little prince who inhabited a planet so tiny he could watch them at will. By moving his chair a few inches at a time, he once enjoyed forty-four sunsets in one day.

On August 23, 1966, an unmanned floating camera, controlled by an American research station in Hampton, Virginia, recorded the first shadowy image of earth rising above the crest of a pockmarked moon. But it wasn't until December 1968 that humans were dazzled with this exquisite, full-color view of an earthrise. It was Christmas Eve, a fitting moment to contemplate the stars and the planets and the beckoning darkness beyond. The crew of the spaceship *Apollo 8* – William Anders, Frank Borman, and James Lovell – were the first humans to observe the phenomenon from outer space. Traveling at supersonic speed, circling the moon, *Apollo*'s camera captured this memorable photograph of earth rising majestically above the lunar landscape.

To a world grown weary of the turbulence of the sixties – the assassinations, the Vietnam War, the Cold War, the polluted environment – it seemed a vision of incomparable loveliness. It blazed like a bright star of hope, of mysteries yet to be revealed, of distances yet to be run, of promises yet to be fulfilled.

It was an image to delight even the most cynical, media-battered mind. In a world where it was commonplace to say there was nothing new under the sun, here it came – the world, our world, in all its beauty and glory, as we had never before glimpsed it. A vision of unimaginable sweetness. The power of the photograph to delight, to enchant, to surprise had never been so breathtakingly demonstrated.

Saint-Exupéry's little prince would have applauded the enthusiasm of the American astronauts in the lunar sweep that gave them this spectacular view of their fragile planet, rising in all its sublime majesty and glory. What Nadar's aerial photographs had done for earthbound Parisians in 1858, the astronauts did for the world more than a century later.

1968
EARTHRISE

WILLIAM ANDERS / AMERICAN 1933–

Sources

Grateful acknowledgement is made to the following institutions and individuals for permission to reproduce the photographs.

1 View of the Courtyard: Gernsheim Collection, Harry Ransom Humanities Research Center, University of Texas at Austin

2 Latticed Window: Trustees of the Science Museum, London

3 Boulevard du Temple: Bayerisches Nationalmuseum, Munich

4 Colossus of Ramses II: International Museum of Photography at George Eastman House, Rochester

5 Aerial View of Paris: Bibliothèque Nationale, Paris

6 Abraham Lincoln: The Library of Congress, Prints and Photographs Division, Washington, D.C.

7 Mrs. Herbert Duckworth: International Museum of Photography at George Eastman House, Rochester

8 Old Faithful: The Denver Public Library, Western History Department, Denver

9 Galloping Horse: International Museum of Photography at George Eastman House, Rochester

10 Chief Sitting Bull: Notman Archives, McCord Museum, Montreal

11 Gathering Water-lilies: International Museum of Photography at George Eastman House, Rochester

12 George Eastman with Kodak Camera: International Museum of Photography at George Eastman House, Rochester

13 Underwater Self-portrait: Courtesy of Ruth L. Dugan, Philadelphia

14 Child Spinner: International Museum of Photography at George Eastman House, Rochester

15 Charlie Chaplin(TM) © Copyright Bubbles Inc. S.A. 1989. Represented by Bliss House, Inc., Springfield, Massachusetts 01103

16 Charles Lindbergh and the *Spirit of St. Louis*: Canapress Photo Service, Toronto, Ontario

17 Greta Garbo: Courtesy of John Kobal, Kobal Collection, London

18 Drop of Milk: Courtesy of Dr. Harold Edgerton, Massachusetts Institute of Technology, Cambridge, Massachusetts

19 Sharecropper Family: The Library of Congress, Prints and Photographs Division, Washington, D.C.

20 Migrant Mother: The Library of Congress, Prints and Photographs Division, Washington, D.C.

21 Jesse Owens: Canapress Photo Service, Toronto, Ontario

22 Death of a Loyalist Soldier: Courtesy of Cornell Capa, Executor, Robert Capa Estate, New York

23 The Bombing of Guernica: Canapress Photo Service, Toronto, Ontario

24 Franklin Delano Roosevelt: Canapress Photo Service, Toronto, Ontario

25 Pearl Harbor: Canapress Photo Service, Toronto, Ontario

26 Winston Spencer Churchill: Courtesy Yousuf Karsh, Ottawa; © 1941

27 The Warsaw Ghetto Uprising: Canapress Photo Service, Toronto, Ontario

28 D Day: Courtesy Gilbert A. Milne, Toronto, Ontario

29 Raising the Flag at Iwo Jima: Associated Press photo from Canapress Photo Service, Toronto, Ontario

30 The Living Dead of Buchenwald: *Life* Magazine; © Time Inc.

31 Anne Frank: Canapress Photo Service, Toronto, Ontario

32 First Atomic Bomb Explosion: Los Alamos National Laboratory

33 The Walk to Paradise Garden: Black Star, New York

34 Gandhi: *Life* Magazine; © Time Inc.

35 Unidentified Flying Object: J. Allen Hynek Center for UFO Studies, Lima, Ohio

36 Marilyn Monroe: Canapress Photo Service, Toronto, Ontario

37 Ranch Market: Courtesy of Robert Frank, Mabou, Nova Scotia

38 Mao Tse-tung: Courtesy of the Embassy of the People's Republic of China, Ottawa, Ontario

39 Cuban Missile Base: Canapress Photo Service, Toronto, Ontario

40 The March on Washington: Canapress Photo Service, Toronto, Ontario

41 John Fitzgerald Kennedy, Jr.: UPI/Bettman Newsphotos, New York

42 Execution of a Viet Cong Suspect: Associated Press photo from Canapress Photo Service, Toronto, Ontario

43 Shooting at Kent State University: Copyright 1970, Valley Daily News, Tarentum, Pennsylvania

44 South Vietnamese Children Burned by Napalm: Associated Press photo from Canapress Photo Service, Toronto, Ontario

45 Tomoko in Her Bath: Black Star, New York

46 Terry Fox: Courtesy of Gail Harvey, Toronto, Ontario

47 Edwin "Buzz" Aldrin on the Moon: NASA Lyndon B. Johnson Space Center

48 Harp Seal Pup: Courtesy of Fred Bruemmer, Montreal, Quebec

49 The *Challenger* Explodes: NASA Lyndon B. Johnson Space Center

50 The Statue of Liberty: Ellis Island Foundation, New York

51 Earthrise: NASA Lyndon B. Johnson Space Center

Every effort has been made to secure copyright details and related permission. Additional information will be welcomed by the publisher.

TYPESETTING:	Attic Typesetting Inc.
PRODUCTION ART:	Universal Communications
	Eleonore Richter
DUOTONES &	
COLOUR SEPARATION:	Colour Technologies
PAPER:	Friesen Matte/80 lb.
PRINTING AND	
BINDING:	D. W. Friesen & Sons Ltd.
DESIGN:	V. John Lee